The Little Book of Doctor Rules

Reprinted by special arrangement with Square One Publishers, Garden City Park, New York, U.S.A.

First Indian Edition, Published in 2024 by:

Embassy Book Distributors
120, Great Western Building, Maharashtra Chamber of Commerce Lane, Fort, Mumbai 400 023, India
Tel: (+9122) -30967415, 22819546
Email: info@embassybooks.in
www.embassybooks.in

ISBN: 978-93-92217-76-0

Distribution Centres:
Mumbai, Ahmedabad, Bangalore, Kolkata, Chennai, Hyderabad, New Delhi, Pune

Cover Design by Rishikumar Thakur for Embassy Book Distributors

Printed at SAP Print Solutions Pvt. Ltd., Mumbai

Contents

Acknowledgments

In my book *Twentieth Century Men in Medicine: Personal Reflections,* I talked about my training with eight of my mentors. Many of the rules in this book come from the influences of these men, whom I would like to thank for shaping my professional mindset in clinical medicine.

Of the four Vanderbilt medical school professors on this list, John Shapiro taught me pathology at the autopsy table, Robert Hartman illuminated the details of hematology, Rudolph Kampmeier was the master of the physical examination and diagnostic process, and Elliot Newman demonstrated the need to doubt and question every finding.

During my post-graduate years, Robert Loeb, chief of my residency at Columbia-Presbyterian, insisted on a science of medicine and a scientific use of medication. David Rogers, my chief of medicine at Vanderbilt, showed me the art of bedside medicine. Grant Liddle, my mentor in an endocrinology fellowship, taught me the scientific method of inquiry.

Finally, Tinsley Harrison, chair of medicine at the University of Alabama at Birmingham, showed me the value of having patients keep diaries to uncover hidden causes of symptoms.

Many of the rules in this book come also from colleagues, classmates, and friends who taught me much. I thank them all. I wish I

could remember which rules came from which people, but those memories are now a blur in my mind.

I would also like to thank my wife, renowned portrait artist Ann Cowden, who provided editorial assistance and encouragement at every step.

Introduction

Since graduating from Vanderbilt University School of Medicine in 1955, I have witnessed many changes in the practice of medicine. The most dramatic changes have been the marked increase in specialists and the equally marked decrease in generalists—those physicians and other healthcare professionals in first-contact medical care, by which I mean general internists, family physicians, general practitioners, pediatricians, and nurse practitioners. These professionals see patients as they enter the healthcare system. At this initial point in the process, the nature and cause of a clinical problem is unknown.

From my experience in primary care, and from discussions with colleagues, I have found that over 50 percent of primary care patients do not have a definable medical disease. They have complaints or symptoms but no medical disease. Nevertheless, while there may not a definable medical disease to explain every symptom, every symptom has a definable cause. Uncovering these hidden causes takes careful listening, observation, and a collaborative, trusting relationship between professional and patient. Identifying these hidden causes is the essential role of primary care and a major focus of the rules in this book.

While this book is aimed mainly at those in primary care, it is meant to be used by all healthcare professionals. Divided into six

parts, it contains rules for developing patient rapport, the diagnostic process, mental status examination, the use of medication, caring for difficult patients, and being a professional. These rules provide guidance on how to learn the details of a patient's lived life, establish a trusting relationship with a patient, and address the concerns of a patient. By seeing each patient as a human being instead of a collection of symptoms, healthcare workers of every variety can significantly improve the healthcare system, benefitting not only patients but also themselves.

I
Rules for Developing Patient Rapport

1

The interview is the beginning of treatment.

2

Learn to listen to the life story of a patient. Health conditions tend to arise from a person's lived life.

3

Sit down when you talk with a patient. Don't talk with a patient while you keep one hand on the door.

4

While listening to a patient, do not do anything else. Just listen.

Let the young know they will never find a more interesting, more instructive book than the patient himself.

—Giorgio Baglivi

5

Let a patient ramble on for at least five minutes at the outset of an interview. You will learn a lot.

6

There is no substitute for direct observation.

7

Learn to watch a patient's facial expressions.

8

Always face a patient. Maintain eye contact but do not stare. Some people cannot tolerate very much eye contact, so you may have to look out of the corners of your eyes.

9

Notice the change in a patient's respiratory rate as you discuss different subjects. Watch the top edge of the shoulders move with each breath.

10

If a patient's eyes are moving as you talk, that patient is not paying full attention to what is being said.

11

It is impossible to think and listen simultaneously. Listen. Think. Listen. Think.

12

Talk with patients, not to them.

13

Adjust your pace to the pace of your patient.

14

Inquire about touchy subjects by using statements instead of questions. For example, say, "I am wondering how much alcohol you drink each day," instead of asking, "How much alcohol do you drink daily?" A patient will find a statement less intrusive than a question.

If I set out to prove something, I am no real scientist—I have to learn to follow where the facts lead me—I have to learn to whip my prejudices.

LAZZARO SPALLANZANI

15

Whatever subject a patient is most comfortable discussing is probably not the real trouble.

16

Listen carefully when a patient begins a comment by saying, "This may not be important, but . . ."

17

Most patients can tell you why they got sick.

18

Most patients can tell you what their sicknesses are.

19

Give a patient permission to discuss unusual behavior. Do this in a specific manner. For example, if you think a patient may be abusing laxatives, say, "Some people take a laxative once in a while; some people take a number of laxatives every day. Which group would you fall into?"

20

Always examine the part that hurts.

21

Avoid "organ" talk. Do not ask, "How is your stomach?" or "How is your heart?" Do not let patients use organ talk either. Insist on a language of symptoms, feelings, and thoughts.

22

If a patient talks about a diagnosis, ask about the diagnosis. In other words, if a patient says, "It started as the flu," ask, "What was that flu like?"

23

Use nonspecific language. General inquiries produce informative answers, while specific questions require "yes or no" answers and produce limited information. In other words, say, "Tell me about your breathing," instead of asking, "Have you ever had any shortness of breath?"

24

Listen to what a patient is not telling you.

Blessed is he who carries within himself a God, an ideal, and who obeys it: Ideal of art, ideal of science, ideal of the gospel virtues, therein lie the springs of great thoughts and great actions; they all reflect light from the Infinite.

—Louis Pasteur

25

If a patient says, "I can't talk about that," in response to a certain question, take a shockingly wild guess to break the ice. For example, if the question was about a patient's spouse, take a wild guess that the spouse is a convicted felon or something equally improbable. If your guess is confirmed, you will appear insightful, which may cause the patient to talk more freely about the subject. If your guess is denied, it will likely be so much worse than reality that the patient will feel relieved and thus more able to talk about the subject. The subject is defused either way.

26

Never appear shocked by anything a patient tells you.

27

It is all right for a patient to get angry, cry, laugh, or express any other feeling.

28

Silence can be helpful. Wait for a patient to break it. It is likely something very important will be said.

29

Occasionally, a difficult patient may be won over by a compliment.

30

Be standing when a patient enters or leaves your office.

31

Do not back out of the room as you are talking with a patient.

32

The last statement a patient makes at the end of an appointment may be very important.

33

Never leave the room
while a patient is talking.

34

Do not talk to an angry patient about any other subject until you understand the source of the anger. Take as long as necessary to defuse the anger.

II
Rules for the Diagnostic Process

35

When trying to reach a diagnosis, you will likely have to throw out at least one finding. Choose wisely that which you discard.

36

There is no single blood or urine test that can differentiate a well person from a sick person.

37

The only way to determine if a person is well or sick is to listen, look carefully, and ask good questions.

38

Do not go on "fishing expeditions" for diseases that are not dictated by a patient's history, a patient's physical examination, or the circumstances of a patient's case. If you do, expect false positives.

39

If a patient does not get better after receiving a diagnosis and beginning treatment, be willing to throw out the diagnosis and start over.

40

There is no objective method to measure the presence or absence of pain.

41

There is no objective method to measure a patient's pain level.

42

Rare manifestations of common diseases are more prevalent than common manifestations of rare diseases.

43

Absence of clinical evidence is not evidence of its absence.

You must always be students, learning and unlearning till your life's end, and if, gentlemen, you are not prepared to follow your profession in this spirit, I implore you to leave its ranks and betake yourself to some third-class trade.

—Joseph Lister

44

Symptoms attributable to medical diseases tend to get better or worse. Symptoms attributable to psychological disorders tend to stay about the same over time.

45

When caring for a very sick patient, doubt the results of all tests.

46

Consider ordering a sed rate. It is a useful test when used wisely.

47

Use laboratory tests one at a time and with precision.

48

Be careful with labels. They can be very difficult to remove.

49

No organ system fails in isolation.

50

Any lump found by a patient is probably more clinically significant than one found by a physician. (An exception to this rule would be a self-discovered calcified xiphoid process, sometimes reported as a tumor by middle-aged men in a panic.)

51

All recurring symptoms are triggered by something. Find out what the trigger is.

52

There is no substitute for data.

53

Measure, measure, measure.
Observe, observe, observe.

54

Curiosity is not a reason to order a test. It kills not only cats but also diagnostic accuracy.

55

Normal diagnostic limits are not absolute truths. They are simply statistically derived values. At least 2.5 percent of the public live healthy and long lives above the upper limit of any test, and at least 2.5 percent of the public live healthy and long lives below the lower limit of any test.

56

A drug screen does not test for all known drugs.

57

Do not make the error of accepting the first abnormality found as the cause of a patient's symptoms.

58

You cannot diagnose what is not in your differential diagnosis.

The reason why many diseases are unknown to the Greek physicians is because they are ignorant of the whole, to which attention ought to be paid, for the part can never be well unless the whole is well.

—Plato

59

The pathophysiology of a diagnosed disease should explain a patient's symptoms. If it does not, then either your diagnosis is wrong or you have overlooked a second disease that could explain the symptoms.

60

A patient under the age of fifty who has several symptoms likely has only one health condition.

61

A patient over the age of fifty who has several symptoms likely has more than one health condition.

62

If you are unsure of a patient's health condition, do not say, "I don't know what you have." Say, "I don't know what you have yet."

63

Solving a difficult diagnostic puzzle as a consultant requires the ability to study the details of a workup and uncover the diseases that were missed. You are looking for something that was not done.

64

A careful and detailed occupational history can be helpful in solving a patient's diagnostic puzzle.

The desire to take medicine is perhaps the greatest feature which distinguishes man from animals.

—Sir William Osler

65

When you evaluate a seriously ill patient, shape your list of possibilities to treatable diseases, even if they are rare.

66

A detailed dietary history can be helpful in a patient who displays symptoms of unknown origin. Ask what such a patient ate at each meal over the past three days.

67

If you order a test that has a high probability of returning a false positive, inform the patient ahead of time that you may need to do this test a second or even a third time before you can trust the outcome. Do not discuss any results until you are confident in the information.

68

Do not discount the possibility of protein malnutrition or another form of dietary deficiency, regardless of a patient's weight.

69

Masses are either palpable or they are not. There is no such thing as a suggestion of a mass.

70

Once a physician and patient agree on a diagnosis of a chronic disease, the diagnosis becomes nearly impossible to reverse, whether it is accurate or not.

As to diseases, make a habit of two things: to help or at least to do no harm.
—Hippocrates

71

The assumption of a purely localized disease process in a systemic disease is a common error. For example, edema in hyperthyroidism, or constipation in hypercalcemia.

72

The diagnostic process was not invented to determine if a patient is sick or well; it was developed to determine what kind of sickness is present.

73

Any weight gain or loss that occurs within a ten-day period consists of water weight.

74

Prevalence of serious disease varies widely according to the type of practice. It is low in community or family practice, high in a referral diagnostic center, and very high in a referral critical care unit.

75

Severe acute abdominal pain always requires a surgical consultation.

76

A good surgeon evaluating acute abdominal pain is equivalent to a highly sensitive and specific laboratory test.

77

An acute surgical abdomen is when a good surgeon says it is an acute surgical abdomen. There is no other test as reliable.

78

If you catch yourself thinking a patient might have either hyperthyroidism or hypothyroidism, then it is likely the patient has neither condition.

79

Glass will show on an x-ray.

80

A middle-aged man who suddenly develops what appears to be a character disorder, dysphasia, or some new behavior has a brain tumor until proven otherwise.

81

An obese patient who is consistently losing weight probably has a health condition, even if the patient is on a diet.

82

Pyloric obstruction can be an elusive diagnosis. It can present as constipation or just a feeling of fullness. The classic symptom of vomiting is not always present.

It is a most gratifying sign of the rapid progress of our time that our best textbooks become antiquated so quickly.

—Theodor Billroth

83

Thyrotoxicosis without a palpable thyroid gland is rare. When this circumstance occurs, think of exogenous intake of thyroid hormone.

84

False positive values are a diagnostic pitfall with outpatients in primary care. When a patient is not sick and has come in only for a checkup, discard any positive test result and retest.

85

False negative values are a diagnostic pitfall with the critically ill. When a patient is critically ill, discard any important negative test result and retest.

86

Prevalence is to the diagnostic process as gravity is to the planetary system. It has the power of a physical law. Above all other factors, it controls the accuracy of the diagnostic process.

III
Rules for Mental Status Examination

87

There is no blood or urine test to measure mental function and there may never be.

88

If in doubt regarding the presence of dementia, do a mental status evaluation.

My determination is not to remain stubbornly with my ideas, but I'll leave them and go over to others as soon as I am shown plausible reasons which I can grasp.

—Antonie van Leeuwenhoek

89

It is not uncommon to miss a diagnosis of dementia in a hospitalized patient. This error tends to occur when a cognitive mental status evaluation has been omitted.

90

Social skills are the last thing to be lost in relation to dementia. Do not be fooled by a patient's ability to be pleasant, sociable, or carry on a polite conversation.

91

Some patients with dementia will do everything possible to hide their disorientation, including reading the date of a nearby newspaper when being tested for time orientation.

92

Restlessness can result from hypoxemia. Remember this fact, especially when an elderly person gets restless at night.

93

A time orientation test must include inquiries into the day of the week, the day of the month, the month, and the year.

94

The first clue of dementia may be confusion at night.

In the fields of observation, chance favors only the prepared mind.
—LOUIS PASTEUR

95

Assume that the acute onset of confusion in an elderly person is the result of infection.

96

Learn how to do a thorough mental status evaluation. Do this evaluation while you perform a general patient examination, noting your observations of a patient's mood, affect, attitude, appearance, speech content, delusions, hallucinations, judgment, memory (both recent and remote), etc., in the patient's case notes afterwards.

IV
Rules for the Use of Medication

97

Know which abnormality or symptom you are going to follow during treatment. Choose one you can measure.

98

If there is no abnormality or symptom to follow, do not treat a patient with medicine or surgery.

He [Dr. David Gruby] was called to a paralyzed patient. He found her immobilized in her armchair. "What oil do you use in your kitchen? Can I see it?" When the bottle was produced, Gruby uncorked it and calmly began emptying it on the carpet. The patient jumped up: "Here, that's a Persian rug." The rug was ruined—the lady cured.

—Gustav Monod

99

If a drug is not working, cease its use.

100

If a drug is working, maintain its use.

101

When treating an acutely ill patient, do not change anything if the patient is getting better.

102

If changes in drug treatment are necessary, change only one drug at a time if possible.

103

Stop drug use in treatment whenever possible. If impossible, cease a patient's use of as many drugs as possible whenever possible.

104

Never treat a drug reaction with another drug unless this second drug is a proven antidote to the first.

105

Use as few drugs in treatment as possible.

106

Medicine should make a patient feel better, not worse. (This rule does not apply to a patient receiving chemotherapy.)

107

If a drug makes a patient feel worse, stop its use and find a suitable alternative. (This rule does not apply to a patient receiving chemotherapy.)

108

When a patient is taking medications about which you are ignorant, research these medications and then cease the patient's use of as many of them as possible.

109

There is no such thing as an organ-specific drug. All drugs affect the entire body.

A hypochondriac was advised by Sydenham to consult a physician in Inverness. The man proceeded on horseback; he could not find the doctor; he returned very angry but cured. "Nothing," said Sydenham, "so cherishes and strengthens the blood and spirits as riding a horse."

—Sir Andrew Macphail

110

Do not get your drug information exclusively from drug company representatives.

111

When taking a detailed drug history, start with the drugs taken that day, then the day before, and then the day before that.

112

Do not treat acute anxiety with drugs except in real emergencies.

113

"Little d" depression is a normal part of grief or worry. It passes. Do not treat "little d" depression with drugs.

114

"Big D" depression is a disease that requires antidepressant drugs, the dosages of which have been determined carefully according to need.

115

Inform patients who are taking antidepressants that they must take their medications consistently, not just when they feel depressed.

116

The progress of many symptoms (for example, pain or depression) can be measured with the use of a self-rating scale from 0 to 10.

117

Learn which drugs require titration of dosage.

118

If a patient gets sick while taking multiple drugs, one or more of the drugs is causing the symptoms. If possible, cease the use of these medications and observe the patient. (This rule does not apply to a patient receiving chemotherapy.)

119

Few, if any, pharmaceuticals cannot be safely eliminated from treatment.

I have learned at least three principles . . . not to take authority when I can have facts, not to guess when I can know, not to think a man must take physic because he is sick.

—Oliver Wendell Holmes

120

Learn which pharmaceuticals should be slowly tapered off instead of being abruptly discontinued in treatment.

121

Learn the difference between titration and tapering.

122

Do not give a drug intravenously or intramuscularly if it can be given orally. (Although there is at least one exception to this rule: Intravenous narcotics in a patient with severe pain from an acute myocardial infarction.)

The most important difference between a good and indifferent clinician lies in the amount of attention paid to the story of a patient.

—Sir Farquhar Buzzard

123

Never use a potentially toxic drug when its benefit is minimal or zero.

124

In a patient with acute incapacitating pain, use narcotics intravenously to relieve the pain until the patient is comfortable.

125

Any new abnormality that occurs with the administration of a new drug is due to the drug until proven otherwise.

126

There is no manifestation that cannot be caused by any given medication.

127

There are few clinical trials of patients taking more than four drugs, and very few of patients taking three.

128

For a patient with chronic pain, no matter how severe, do not use narcotics unless the patient has a terminal disease. Then use all that is needed to relieve the pain.

129

The likelihood of an adverse drug reaction rises considerably with an increase in the number of drugs administered.

130

The absence of a reported specific toxicity of a drug does not mean toxicity cannot occur.

131

Drug reactions can be unique to a patient.

132

Enemas, sedatives, or the use of multiple drugs can cause nighttime falls.

133

Elderly people can be fragile and tire easily. Perform diagnostic workups on such patients gently.

134

Learn which treatments are incapable of producing a useful result. If a treatment is incapable of producing a useful result, do not use it.

135

There are more people taking thyroid hormone who do not need it than people taking it who need it.

The doctor may . . . learn more about the illness from the way the patient tells the story than from the story itself.

—James Bryan Herrick

136

If you doubt a drug will work, you are probably right.

137

Patients often take pharmaceuticals from several physicians simultaneously.

138

If you add a drug to a patient's treatment, try to remove one.

139

Be on the alert for hypnotic-sedative abuse, particularly in older patients. Such abuse is often denied. Look out for withdrawal symptoms, such as seizure, which can serve as clues.

140

Patients frequently do not take pharmaceuticals as prescribed.

141

On each return visit, ask an elderly patient who is taking several pharmaceuticals to describe the color, size, and name of each pill or capsule; the time of day each dose is taken; and the number of each pill or capsule taken. The few minutes it takes to acquire this information will save you hours of problems later.

What the mind doesn't handle is relegated to the body, so if the mind doesn't take it in, whatever it is, then it's going to produce a physical symptom.

—WILLIAM MUNDY

142

If a patient uses a prescription drug for several months, the patient will usually be on it for a lifetime unless a physician stops its use.

143

The less often a patient has to take a particular medication, the more likely each dose will be taken properly.

V
Rules for Caring for Difficult Patients

144

Be wary of patients who smile when they describe pain, severe symptoms, misfortunes in life, or the failures of doctors to help so far. A patient who responds in one way verbally and another nonverbally is conflicted or confused.

145

Be wary of hysterical patients. They may have several diseases.

146

You cannot be everyone's physician.

Of all the technical aids which increase the doctor's power of observation, none comes even close in value to the skillful use of spoken words—the words of the doctor and the words of the patient.

—Brian Bird

147

Learn to distinguish between the patients whose physician you can be and the patients whose physician you cannot be.

148

Provide patients whose physician you cannot be with referrals to other doctors. You may explain this choice to a patient by saying, "I do not have the training to care for your problem."

149

If you do not know what is wrong with a patient after you have taken a history, then take another history. If you still do not know what is wrong, then take a third history. If you still do not know what is wrong, then it is unlikely you ever will.

150

Never tell a symptomatic patient, "Don't worry. It's all in your head." It is demeaning and insulting.

151

When a patient insists on receiving a diagnosis but you suspect there is no demonstrable medical illness to explain the patient's symptoms, say, "I know what you do not have," and then slowly list every disease you know the patient does not have to the point of tedium.

152

When listing the diseases a patient does not have, be sure to include those diseases most feared, especially those that killed close members of the patient's family. Do this only if you have excluded those diseases with absolute certainty, of course.

153

Never reassure a new patient who has expressed multiple complaints of chronic health issues too early about the absence of a specific disease. Wait a few days to do so. There is a greater chance the patient will believe you then.

154

Never tell a symptomatic patient, "There is nothing wrong with you." It is demeaning and insulting.

The relationship between doctor and patient partakes of a peculiar intimacy. It presupposes on the part of the physician not only knowledge of his fellow men, but sympathy. He sits, not as a judge of morals or of conduct, but rather as an impersonal repository for confession. The patient, on his part, must feel the need of aid, and few patients come to the doctor except with this incentive.

—WARFIELD T. LONGCOPE

155

Anger, when repressed, is often associated with depression.

156

The problems of some patients are beyond existing medical knowledge.

157

If a patient has multiple chronic symptoms and jumps from one symptom to another in conversation, label several chairs in the exam room according to body part (e.g., "head," "legs," "chest," "stomach," etc.) and ask the patient to sit in the appropriate chair when talking about each one. After a few chair changes, the patient will likely reveal what the real problem is and drop all mention of symptoms.

158

Presume any juvenile diabetic patient with recurrent ketoacidosis is not taking insulin as required until proven otherwise. While confronting such a patient is rarely helpful, knowledge of this rule can be.

159

Poisoning or factitious disease should be considered in connection with any patient who remains undiagnosed. Test for poisoning before you discuss the subject with a patient.

160

Factitious disease should be considered in connection with any patient who has unusual findings, especially when the patient is a healthcare worker or spouse of a healthcare worker.

Blessed is the physician who takes a good history, looks keenly at his patient and thinks a bit.

—WALTER C. ALVAREZ

161

Paired or butterfly-shaped bruises are caused by pinching and are usually self-inflicted.

162

Certain medications taken by a patient's close relatives may be clues to a factitious disease. Examples include insulin and anticoagulants.

163

Factitious fever does not elevate heart rate.

Thank God every morning when you get up that you have something to do which must be done, whether you like it or not. Being forced to work, and forced to do your best, will breed in you temperance, self-control, diligence, strength of will, content, and a hundred of other virtues which the idle never know.

—Charles Kingsley

164

Self-inflicted skin lesions do not appear between the shoulder blades.

165

A patient with a factitious disease will not remain with the physician who made the diagnosis.

166

Factitious disease can result from collaboration. For example, collaboration between patient and friend, patient and parent, or patient and spouse.

167

Be wary of a patient who has had multiple surgeries.

168

Be wary of patients who say they are allergic to everything.

169

Be wary of patients who say they cannot take any drugs.

170

Be wary of patients who complain of gas in anatomical locations that could not possibly be affected by gas.

171

Some psychotic patients may present with physical symptoms. Symptoms attributable to psychosis often have unusual or bizarre descriptions, such as water running out of the ears, drippings from the fingers, pain like a belt choking the brain, or itchy teeth.

Without scientific knowledge, a compassionate wish to serve mankind's health is meaningless, and it should be possible to acknowledge the triumphs of medicine without denigrating the art.

—Herrman Blumgart

172

Alcohol on a patient's breath does not mean the patient is an alcoholic or even that the patient is intoxicated.

173

Never refer to a patient in pejorative terms. Doing so only reveals your inability to understand the world of another person.

174

Some diseases are idiosyncratic to a patient.

175

There are difficult physicians just as there are difficult patients. We are all only human after all.

176

There will always be some patients who seem to want your help but won't let you help them.

VI
Rules for Being a Professional

177

Much disease is self-inflicted, consciously or not.

178

Most office patients in primary care get well with or without you.

The trouble with doctors is not that they don't know enough, but that they don't see enough.

—Sir Dominic J. Corrigan

179

In order to be a good clinician, you must know what you do not know.

180

The absence of a demonstrable medical disease in a symptomatic patient does not automatically point to a diagnosis of mental illness.

181

The presence of a demonstrable medical disease in a symptomatic patient does not rule out mental illness.

182

Violation of either of the previous two rules is often a cause of error.

183

You do not have to like a patient, but it sure helps if you do.

184

If your dislike of a patient is severe, the patient may be reflecting an aspect of yourself that you dislike.

185

If you still dislike a patient after three visits, refer the patient to someone else.

186

All patients will lie about something.
Some will lie about everything.

187

If a patient is clearly lying to you, remember that the lie is usually addressed to you as a doctor, not a person.

188

No patient's lie should be held against a patient or provoke anger in you.

189

Lies can be important medical symptoms.

190

Respect every employee at your place of business, no matter the job. These are the people who make it possible for you to be a physician.

191

Odds are high of a physician burning out, becoming an addict, getting divorced, or even committing suicide. Find out why before one of these outcomes happens to you.

192

Know the things you can change. Know the things you cannot change. Develop the wisdom to recognize the difference.

Not for the self, not for the fulfillment of any worldly desire or gain, but solely for the good of suffering humanity, I will treat my patients and excel all.

—CHARAKA

193

Just because you know a lot of physiology, biochemistry, and anatomy does not mean you know anything about people.

194

Let your patients teach you.

195

Learn something from every patient you meet.

196

Do not refer to a patient by the organ affected by illness, as in, "the gallbladder in room 3," or "the kidney in room 5."

197

There is no such thing as an uninteresting patient. Each can be fascinating in some way if you take the time to discover what that way is.

198

If you do not like clinical medicine, get out of it today.

199

Learn to say, "No," but say it tactfully.

200

Do not discuss your personal life with patients.

201

Be wary of flirtatious patients and learn to deal with them in a straightforward manner. If a patient continues behaving in this manner, refer the patient to another physician.

202

Never have a sexual relationship with a patient or office employee.

203

Many general physicians under-treat depression but over-treat anxiety. Both conditions, however, can be passing phases of the human condition.

204

Many patients will not have demonstrable medical diseases but they will have symptoms.

205

If you cannot identify the condition of a sick patient after a thorough workup, get a consultation.

206

If you cannot identify the condition of a sick patient after getting a consultation, get another consultation.

It is much more important that pertinent information be recorded in the doctor's mind than on a card or in a file.

—Brian Bird

207

If you cannot identify the condition of a sick patient after getting more than one consultation, refer the patient to a well-known medical center.

208

A consultant should discuss a recommendation only with the referring physician and not with the patient.

209

Some diseases are not treatable, but all patients can be given care.

210

Develop a list of physicians you trust and respect, nurture your relationship with them, and contact them about difficult cases. Try to acquaint yourself with at least one trusted physician in each specialty.

211

There are only three ways to answer a question: “I don’t know;” “I don’t know, but I’ll guess;” and “I know.”

212

If you are with an older patient and need time to think, ask for a description of the patient's bowel habits.

213

Almost all sick patients look ill, sound ill, and act ill. A few sick patients look well, sound well, and act well. A few people without disease can look ill, sound ill, and act ill. Be mindful of these possibilities.

214

Time is the greatest diagnostician. Use it wisely.

215

Learn to identify both the placebo-related aspects and the pharmacologically related aspects of a treatment. Keep the two separated in your clinical thinking.

216

There is always a placebo effect in action.

217

All patients, no matter who they may be, want magic from you. Magic does not require pills or surgery.

218

If all you listen to are symptoms, then all you will hear from your patients are symptoms.

219

There are three kinds of patients: Those who believe every word you say and do everything you suggest; those who reflect on what you say, ask you questions, and then make up their own minds about what to do; and those who disagree with everything you say, oppose every suggestion you make, and state that nothing will help them. Learn how to deal with all three.

220

To those patients who believe every word you say and do everything you suggest, be careful what you say and suggest.

221

For those patients who reflect on what you say, ask you questions, and then make up their own minds about what to do, answer all questions.

222

To those patients who disagree with everything you say, oppose every suggestion you make, and state that nothing will help them, express some doubt about the treatments you are suggesting, leading such patients to argue that these treatments will work.

223

Like it or not, there is a little "witch doctor" in all physicians. Use this aspect of yourself wisely and only for the benefit of your patients.

224

Teach patients to be well,
not simply "not sick."

225

There are two types of obese people: Those who are obese from childhood and those who gain weight later in life. There is a very different prognosis for sustained weight loss for each of these two types.

Patients are gold mines of information to a doctor who's willing to listen.

—Sydney Walker III

226

Let a patient know if you have made a mistake in diagnosis or treatment, no matter how small or large the error. Say you are sorry and explain what the patient can expect to happen.

227

There are a number of different body types. Weight and height tables are not absolute truths when it comes to health.

228

Treat the disease a patient has, not the disease you want a patient to have.

229

Do not tell a patient bad news until you are as certain as possible of the accuracy of the finding.

230

Try to leave each patient smiling, no matter how grim the circumstances.

231

With seriously or terminally ill patients, be wary of out-of-town family members, who may cause you headaches. Some call this rule the "out-of-town sibling rule."

232

Never take away hope.

233

Never try to predict exactly how long a patient has to live.

234

You are a patient's advocate. You work for no one else.

235

Avoid any meetings in which an ex-spouse, present spouse, or romantic partner is present.

236

If a patient's spouse refuses to leave the room and makes every effort to prevent you from talking to the patient alone, make sure to find a way to speak to the patient alone.

237

Never examine a patient of the opposite gender without a chaperone.

238

Never let a patient die with a rare but treatable disease.

239

Do not worry about missing a diagnosis of an untreatable disease.

240

Learn how to perform a detailed and thorough neurological examination.

241

Become an expert on what is and what is not a Babinski response.

242

A sign is either "present" or "absent." A sign is never "positive" or "negative."

243

Avoid use of the terms "negative" or "normal" in describing a physical examination.

244

Describe what you see, hear, or feel, and what you do not.

The physician is Nature's assistant.

—GALEN

245

No verbal presentation of a case should ever take more than five minutes. A longer presentation means you do not know what you are talking about.

246

Do not say, "In my experience," until you have been in practice at least ten years. Even then, use the phrase sparingly or not at all.

247

Always check a patient's laboratory and other test results for the correct name. Results can get mislabeled.

248

Human biology and clinical medicine are not the same discipline. Human biologists and clinicians use very different thought processes.

249

Much of what is called "aging" is simply disuse and inactivity.

250

Gently push elderly patients to walk and stretch all their muscles daily.

251

Make a list of deadly but treatable conditions and vow never to miss a diagnosis of any of them. Be sure to include the following illnesses and add others as necessary:

- Addison's disease
- Benign resectable tumors of the brain or spinal cord
- Cryptic blood loss
- Dehydration
- Diabetic ketoacidosis or any acidosis
- Heart failure due to arteriovenous fistulas or other high-output states
- Hyperosmolar states
- Hyperparathyroidism
- Hypoglycemia, especially cases due to hyperinsulinism
- Hypoxemia
- Mechanical intestinal obstruction
- Mechanical pulmonary obstruction
- Meningitis (all types)
- Obstructive renal failure
- Rocky Mountain spotted fever
- Ruptured viscus
- Sepsis
- Subdural hematoma
- Surgically curable forms of hypertension
- Thyrotoxicosis
- Toxic shock

252

Language is the most important tool a physician has. Respect it.

253

Learn to trust your feelings. They can tell you a lot about the emotional state of your patient. If you feel depressed, your patient may be depressed. If you feel confused, your patient may be confused.

254

Don't get angry at your patients if they don't improve with therapy.

255

If a patient asks about the possibility of being sent to a particular well-known clinic, show your wisdom and concern by referring the patient there.

256

Don't get angry at your patients for any reason. If you do, get some help.

257

Learn how often each of your patients needs to return to see you. Some patients require weekly visits, some monthly, some quarterly, and some every year or two. There is no rule of thumb to help you in this matter.

258

Use language correctly and speak concisely.

259

If you do not have a specific diagnosis for a patient who is not seriously ill, it is sometimes better to describe the patient's symptoms physiologically or by using the established names of these symptoms rather than force a diagnosis.

260

In analyzing a patient's stated symptom, keep asking questions until you can make a mental picture of the patient having the symptom.

261

If you cannot imagine how it would feel to have a patient's symptom, you probably do not have an accurate description of the symptom and should ask more questions about its nature.

In the treatment of disease, oftentimes to do nothing is to do everything.

—GIOVANNI BATTISTA MORGAGNI

262

Unless you can repeat what another person has said and have that person nod in agreement, you have not listened accurately. Practice this skill until it becomes second nature.

263

Once you feel you have an accurate understanding of a patient's stated symptom, describe your understanding of the symptom to the patient until the patient agrees (with nodding head) that you grasp what the symptom feels like and the circumstances under which it occurs.

264

Never point or shake your finger at a patient.

265

If a patient gets angry as you talk, then it is likely you said something that angered the patient.

266

If a patient laughs as you talk, then it is likely you said something that was funny to the patient.

267

If a patient cries as you talk, then it is likely you said something that was sad or upsetting to the patient.

268

If a patient begins to argue with you, then it is likely you said something argumentative to the patient.

269

If you do not like a patient's response, consider changing your own behavior.

270

If you find yourself being frequently surprised by the responses of your patients, you may be sending mixed messages—one message with your words, one with your tone of voice, one with your facial expression, one with your body language, etc.

271

A tendency to send mixed messages may be uncovered by an audiovisual recording of your delivery.

272

The first step in effective communication is to gain the full attention of the other person. Sometimes this step requires long periods of silence.

273

Learn how to get the full attention of your patients.

274

Give your patients your full attention.

275

Anger is often a result of fear. Do not respond to a patient's anger defensively. Find out what the patient fears.

276

Do not throw instruments.

277

Speak so you can be heard.

278

Write so others can read what you've written.

279

Doctor's spouses can have medical diseases, too.

280

If you really don't know what
to do, then do nothing.

Frequently, more is accomplished
by treating the person rather
than the disease the patient has.

—James Edgar Paullin

281

Before you examine a patient, warm your hands and stethoscope. If you will be using a speculum, be sure to warm it too.

282

Wash your hands. Do so in front of your patients if possible.

283

Know harm; do not do harm.

284

Always observe a patient's gait.

285

The healthcare system too often teaches a patient to stay sick, not to get well.

286

Be kind to nurses and they will be kind to you.

287

Be unkind to nurses and they may make your life miserable.

288

A hospital is a dangerous place. Use it wisely and as briefly as possible.

289

Never tell a patient, "Don't worry."

290

A bleeding scalp or facial laceration is never as bad as it looks initially.

291

Never wake a patient to administer a sedative or laxative.

292

Confusion is an essential part of learning.

293

The first job of a physician is to determine if a patient is sick or well.

294

Learn about the setting in which a disease has developed. It will tell you much about the diagnosis.

295

A physician's beliefs often determine a patient's beliefs.

296

Warn newly diagnosed patients that they are sure to hear terrifying stories about the same diagnoses. There is always someone who has heard about the same disease, operation, or medicine and will describe the worst possible outcome in relation to it.

297

No one knows how a patient feels but the patient.

298

A physician who treats himself or herself has a fool for a patient and a bigger fool for a physician.

The art of medicine was to be properly learned only from its practice and its exercise.

—Thomas Sydenham

299

The error of making a false diagnosis is often hidden from all parties involved. The patient is satisfied to have a name for the symptoms; the physician has a diagnosis (albeit a false one); the "disease" will always be considered a mild form and will not progress since it does not exist; and treatment may appear to work.

300

In relation to a patient's chronic undiagnosed complaints, have the patient keep a symptom diary. Look for symptom correlations with activities, food, people, work time, and location.

301

Assume a patient with a chronic illness is doing something (albeit unconsciously) to aggravate the symptoms.

302

Assume a patient with a chronic illness is not doing anything (albeit unconsciously) that would alleviate the symptoms.

303

Ask a patient with chronic symptoms two questions: What are you doing that you should stop doing? What are you not doing that you should be doing?

304

All disease labels are abstractions. Only a patient is concrete.

305

Ask your patients what the specialists told them before you tell them what the specialists told you. Doing so will avoid confusion and save you and your patients a lot of time.

306

Stories and metaphors are wonderful teaching devices. To be effective, they must be closely related to the life and world of the patient (i.e., golf stories for golfers, auto repair stories for mechanics, computer-related analogies for IT people, etc.)

307

Reserve resuscitation for witnessed cardiac arrests.

308

Find out who lives in a patent's household.

309

Always act as though an unconscious patient (including one who has been anesthetized) can hear and understand everything you say and will remember what was said.

310

Emotional isolation can lead to illness.

> *The best teaching is that taught by the patient himself.*
>
> —William Osler

311

Balance in life is essential. Pursue an interest outside of medicine.

312

The greater the technology being used, the greater the need for human contact.

313

Your personal qualities can be as important therapeutically as any drug or treatment.

314

If you should inadvertently offend someone, say you are sorry and remember that most people will forgive you eventually.

315

Pay careful attention to patients who say they are going to die.

316

Learn the difference between informed persuasion and informed consent.

317

Do not confuse benign disorders with serious diseases and thereby expose patients to dangerous and unnecessary procedures.

318

If something still has not worked after three attempts, it will never work.

319

Physical distance and emotional distance are not the same.

320

There is an unconscious mind.

321

A response to placebo has no diagnostic significance. Specifically, it does not mean a patient is faking or imagining some illness or symptom, or that the pain is not real.

322

It is more important to know a person than it is to know a person's disease.

323

Never ignore an experienced nurse's observation.

324

The level and intensity of care determine the characteristics of a physician-patient relationship.

325

Each physician is like a drug. With each doctor-patient encounter, a physician's actions can produce side effects, exhibit a duration of action, induce toxicity, be indicated or contraindicated, be supplied in too great or too little in amount, produce a placebo effect, etc. Learn the pharmacology of being a physician.

326

Never ask a patient to do a favor for you.

327

Always leave a diagnostic loophole large enough to crawl back through.

328

The most effective prevention of malpractice is rapport with a patient and complete honesty.

329

What may be considered domineering behavior in an outpatient setting may be considered appropriate behavior in an emergency room setting.

330

No reasonable patient wants autonomy in an emergency or critical care unit. Autonomy will return with recovery from illness.

331

Human perfectibility is an oxymoron.

332

A behavior that is ignored will often extinguish itself.

333

A map of a territory is not the same as the territory. Do not confuse a model with reality.

334

In medicine, anything that can happen will eventually happen.

335

Most patients do not change; they simply change doctors.

336

Use it or lose it. This rule applies to all parts of the body.

337

The appendix is where the surgeon finds it.

338

A patient who prays during an examination is probably gravely ill.

339

Any procedure will take more time to perform than a surgeon says it will.

340

A call from a hospital nurse at night is always a plea for help. Help should always be offered.

341

It takes a real surgeon to stop all bleeds.

342

A consultant, above all else, is a teacher.

343

A symptom is a ticket a patient thinks must be punched in order to see you.

344

Look behind a symptom for the real reason a patient has come to see you.

345

Do not hasten death.

346

Surgery for poorly specified chronic abdominal pain will result in permanent abdominal pain.

347

No matter how much time you have spent explaining a patient's condition, the patient's family will always ask one more question before leaving.

348

Good physicians are like good coaches: They stay on the sidelines and never get in the game.

349

Psychotherapy is sometimes like riding a well-trained horse down a familiar trail to a well-known destination. The gentlest of pressure on the reins keeps the horse on the trail. Only rarely is it necessary to pull the reins one way or the other.

350

The mind readily sees and hears differences. It takes concentration and effort to see or hear similarities.

351

Some patients will not take prescribed drugs because they have not understood their associated instructions. Learn to communicate in a manner these patients can understand.

352

Some patients will not take prescribed drugs because they do not trust your opinion. Learn to build trust and respect with these patients.

353

Some patients will not take prescribed drugs because these medications cause them to feel unwell. Learn to hear these people. They are often correct.

354

As soon as you think you have seen it all, you will encounter something new.

355

Asclepius is said to have spent most of his time keeping his two fighting daughters separated. One was Hygieia, the goddess of prevention. The other was Panacea, the goddess of cure.

356

There is no limit to the strangeness of human behavior.

357

Many people confuse the concept of "life expectancy" with "human life span." Learn the difference between these two ideas.

358

There are three types of questions in clinical judgment: the diagnostic question ("What is wrong?"); the therapeutic question ("What can be done about it?"); and the ethical question ("What should be done about it?")

359

The four fundamental components of good clinical judgment are intelligence, knowledge, experience, continual critical analysis of results.

360

It is usually a second mistake made in response to a first mistake that causes a patient to end up in critical condition.

361

Every era has its chronic fatigue syndrome equivalent. There was "soldier's heart" in World War I; neurasthenia in the 1920s; reactive hypoglycemia in the 1930s and 40s, and again in the 70s; chronic brucellosis in the 1940s and 50s; and so on. There will always be a group of patients who do not feel well, tire easily, and need a large amount of rest.

362

Medical school is not designed to teach you much about life.

363

Time is frequently the best medicine.

364

Medical diseases cannot explain all human misery.

365

Being a physician is a great privilege. Do not abuse it.

Conclusion

As a healthcare professional, it is important to understand that over 50 percent of patients in primary care do not have a definable medical disease. In light of this fact, it is no wonder that false diagnoses are so common, occurring in over 30 percent of patients in primary care. Sincerely hoping to help every patient, doctors can feel a strong need to give every person they evaluate a diagnosis in order to start them on the road to treatment and recovery. Unfortunately, false diagnoses are difficult to remove once they've been assigned.

Avoiding the error of false diagnosis requires intense listening and collaboration with a patient. It is the job of a primary care physician to decide if a patient's symptoms are traceable to a medical disease or not. Although not all symptoms are due to medical diseases, all symptoms have definable causes. Patients do not necessarily require a diagnosis to feel they are being helped; they simply need to know their concerns are being addressed properly. The key to helping every patient is to develop a rapport with them, establish trust with them, learn the details of their lived lives, and listen closely to how these details are given in order to uncover the often hidden causes of their symptoms.

Based on a lifetime of experience in the medical world, the rules you have read throughout this book—from those that deal with

building good relationships with patients, the diagnostic process, and determining a patient's mental status to those that deal with the use of medication, caring for difficult patients, and being a professional—are meant to provide the guidance necessary to address the concerns of patients and improve their experiences within our healthcare system—in other words, the guidance to help patients in a way that has been neglected for too long.

Above all, these rules urge the acceptance of patients as human beings and not merely as collections of symptoms. They form an approach that is invaluable not only to physicians but also to healthcare workers of all kinds, and, as you will soon find, one that benefits both patient and healthcare professional alike.

About the Author

Clifton A. Meador, MD, is a graduate of the Vanderbilt University School of Medicine in Nashville. He trained at Columbia Presbyterian Hospital in New York, where he completed a residency, and at the Vanderbilt University School of Medicine, where he completed an NIH fellowship in endocrinology. After practicing medicine, he joined the faculty of medicine at the University of Alabama, where he was professor of medicine and then dean of the UAB School of Medicine from 1968 to 1973. He then served as chief of medicine and chief medical officer of Saint Thomas Hospital in Nashville from 1973 to 1998. From 1999 to 2012, he served as the first executive director of the Meharry-Vanderbilt Alliance. He is professor of medicine emeritus at both the Vanderbilt School of Medicine and Meharry Medical College. Currently, Dr. Meador and his wife, renowned portrait artist Ann Cowden, live in Nashville, Tennessee.

ISBN: 978-93-55463-64-7

Publisher: Pharos Books (P) Ltd.
Plot No.-55, Main Mother Dairy Road
Pandav Nagar, East Delhi-110092
Phone: 011-40395855, +14049995474
WhatsApp: +91 8368220032
E-mail: sales@pharosbooks.in
Website: www.pharosbooks.in
First Edition: 2022

The New Techniques Requirement for Management
ADARSH KUMAR PANDEY

THE NEW TECHNIQUES REQUIREMENT FOR MANAGEMENT

ADARSH KUMAR PANDEY

Pharos Books